SIGMUND SAYS

A Lighter Look at Freud

Through His Id, Ego and Super-Ego

by Monte Elchoness, Ph.D.

illustrated by Mike Dirham

Monroe Press
Sepulveda, California

Monroe Press
16107 Gledhill Street
Sepulveda, California 91343-2918
(818) 891-6464

Library of Congress Cataloging-in-Publication Data

Elchoness, Monte, 1927-
   Sigmund says: a lighter look at freud through his id, ego, and super-ego
  by Monte Elchoness; illustrated by Mike Dirham. -- 1st ed.
        p.   cm.
  Bibliography: p.
  ISBN 0-936781-04-1 (pbk.)
  1. Psychoanalysis--Popular works. 2. Freud, Sigmund, 1856-1939--Popular works.
  3. Ego (Psychology)--Popular works. 4. Id (Psychology)--Popular works.
  5. Super-ego--Popular works.
  I. Title.
  BF175.E43 1988   150.19'52--dc19   88-4229

Printed in the United States of America
First Edition
10 9 8 7 6 5 4 3 2 1

DEDICATION

It has been written that "Love is a many splendored thing"; to that poetic phrase I add: within the blend of the right partnership. I am thankful that my partner in life and I made our connection, for after nine years of marriage our love for one another and the meaning of our relationship grows stronger and continues to brighten our lives.

I dedicate this book with love to you Dorothy, for without your assistance, support, and ever present love, *Sigmund Says* might have been quite different or not created at all.

I also thank you for helping me keep my personality kids, the id, ego, and super-ego in balance during those times when they sought to play havoc with me. Take joy in *Sigmund Says*, my dear, for it is now a reality, and you have helped to make it so.

ABOUT THE AUTHOR

 Monte Elchoness, Ph.D. is a psychotherapist, author, and a consultant to schools and industry. As a therapist he specializes in family relationships and stress related concerns. As an author he enjoys the challenge of writing about some of our time's more complex issues and presenting them in an easy to understand manner and language. Dr. Elchoness enjoys working with adolescents and writing about their concerns. His connection with youth is important, for he recognizes their need to be understood and accepted, and the difficulty they have in communicating these needs to others. Dr. Elchoness is in demand as a lecturer, and is listed in "Who's Who in California" and "Who's Who in Human Services."

INTRODUCTION

In writing *SIGMUND SAYS*, I present for your consideration my belief that learning, although serious by nature, can also be a fun experience. After all, where is it written (so to speak) that acquiring knowledge must be heavy or painful?

Today, we are becoming more aware of the power of humor and laughter as a healing agent; perhaps as a result of this new understanding, we will also become more open to accepting the value of humor as a tool for learning.

Freud and his work present an excellent example and subject for this project. To begin with, he is acknowledged as an important man of science and a most interesting person. Yet, how many people know much about him or his theories? Whether one accepts his beliefs or not, most would agree, I'm sure, that he has been and continues to be a major contributing influence in the field of psychology and the study of human behavior.

As a psychotherapist, I do not consider myself a Freudian (one who uses Freud's theories exclusively in their work with clients, as in psychoanalysis.) This, however, has not affected or restricted my interest in Freud; for the threads of his influence are plainly seen in the application of all forms of psychology.

A few years ago while in Europe, I made a point of visiting Freud's home and office in Vienna, Austria. This place where he lived and worked is now a most interesting museum containing many of his momentos, photographs and furniture. While there, I felt moved and extremely connected with this man of the past, and what he has helped create.

This book is not meant in any way to make fun of Sigmund Freud or his personality theory. Instead, its purpose is to share an enjoyable experience while conveying factual information about Dr. Freud and some of his beliefs. If some of you more ardent followers of Freud feel I have presented him in a less than respectful manner, I suggest you keep in mind my honorable intentions and that the id within me, like a child seeking pleasure, temporarily took charge. How many people do you know who can say "the id made me do it." For those of you unfamiliar with the id, have patience, hopefully you will be after reading *Sigmund Says.*

Some may consider learning about the id, the ego and the super-ego as complex, dull or even a little scary. As a result of these feelings, one might become resistant to this subject. In this book you will find that the id, ego and super-ego become distinctive character types referred to as "The Personality Kids" and the roles they perform as a part of the personality become quite clear. Perhaps as you learn more about these "Personality Kids," you may even gain some insight into your own personality and the effect it has upon your behavior. Whatever your personal gain from reading this book may be, I hope it includes enjoyment for you and more knowledge about Dr. Freud and his Personality Theory. This was truly a fun project for me; here's hoping you have fun with it too.

Sigmund Freud
1856 - 1939

SIGMUND INTRODUCES HIMSELF

When talking about oneself, it is proper to be somewhat modest; at least that is what I was told on numerous occasions when I was a young boy. Later, I learned if I was to get my views and theories across to the scientific community, I needed to set aside what I was taught about modesty. In dealing with my often resistant and sometimes hostile colleagues it became necessary, as you say in these modern times, to "toot my own whistle" — or is it "horn"?

As I have been given the job of introducing myself in this book, once again I will need to "toot my own whistle." I will attempt to be as accurate with my facts as I can, under the circumstances. The circumstances being that a lot of time has passed and I am getting a little forgetful. After all, I am approaching my 130th birthday, that is I would be if I were still alive.

Starting where I believe one would normally begin (whatever normal is), at my beginning. I was born May 6th, 1856 (under the astrological sign of Taurus, if that is of any interest to you) in a small town called Freiberg, located in Moravia (later called Czechoslovakia) about 150 miles from Vienna. I was much like my father Jakob, (a wool merchant) both physically and also intellectually. In birth order, I was the first born, the eldest child and my mother's favorite. She was a woman, I might add, of excellent taste. At the age of four, my family and I moved to Vienna, where I stayed for close to eighty years.

My goal in life was to become a scientist. I was not interested in practicing medicine, but I entered the University of Vienna medical school anyway, and moving ahead rather quickly, in 1881 I became Dr. Freud. It was difficult for me to advance within the scientific community of the university because of the anti-Semitism in Vienna. Because there was also a need for me to support my wife and six children, I decided to start a medical practice. Specializing in neurology and nervous disorders was my way of satisfying the scientist in me.

As looking back is much easier than looking forward, I could not predict that the hard times which kept me from becoming a scientist at the university would help me at a later date. At least twenty years later as a matter of fact and as a result of my practice of medicine, I experienced my greatest achievement. My accomplishment, it was said, was the most significant of modern science and psychology. I am credited today with having created a dynamic psychology, a study of psychology that involves the transformation of energy within the personality. I used the id, ego and super-ego to represent the three major systems of our personality (that's what this book is all about). The energy that they share and pass to and from each other was how I expressed the organization and dynamics of the human personality. I will tell you more about that later.

From a doctor in Vienna, Joseph Breuer, I learned how "talking out" one's problems and "free-association" (saying whatever comes to one's mind without the prior preparation of one's thoughts) could be used with my patients. Free association became a part of how I did therapy and of psychoanalysis itself. My belief is, the unconscious mind is the storage place for all our problems and is also the place that must be reached for curing disorders of the mind. Through the work I did on myself, with dream and self-analysis of my own unconscious mind, I learned much about what made me tick and I also learned how to improve the treatment of my patients. My book, *The Interpretation of Dreams*, which is much more than a book on dreams, describes my beliefs on the dynamics of the human mind. It took eight years for the first printing (only 600 copies) of this book to be sold, but I did not get discouraged. Today, this book is considered one of the great books of modern times. Not too shabby, as you might say.

My patience finally paid off and I received the recognition I deserved. I never gave up in the pursuit of my work, my theories and what I believed in. It is true, some of my beliefs did change as I grew older and wiser. I am proud that I was flexible enough to revise my theories as a result of my new thoughts and data. Lessons can be learned from my life, beyond my scientific theories. As an example, if one desires success, one needs to be persistent in going after what is wanted. Following through in spite of frustration and disappointment is hard to do, but is necessary if one is to achieve their goals. After all, what scientist hasn't felt some rejection during the process of completing their work. Another important lesson is to remain flexible in your work and your life, for rigid thinking can have a negative effect upon the creative flow of information from the unconscious mind.

In concluding my brief introduction, I will jump many years, to continue my story. In 1937 the Nazis took over Austria and I was most fortunate to escape from Vienna, the city I loved. London became my new home until 1939, the year of my death. It is true, my physical life as we know it ended in my 83rd year, yet, who can deny that I still live on today through the spirit of what I accomplished. And perhaps as a result of *Sigmund Says*, the id, ego and super-ego, which were a significant part of my work, will become familiar and meaningful to you as well. Enjoy what follows as you help Dr. Freud live on.

Once upon a time, as this true story goes, there lived a famous doctor in a faraway land across the sea. I am that famous doctor, und my name is Sigmund Freud.

Join me on a little journey into our minds, so I can tell you about the Id, Ego und Super-Ego und the roles they play in shaping our personalities.

Through something you refer to as movies, I will present their story. Without a doubt, it will be the movie of the century, or perhaps the movie of the moment. In any case, whatever it is it will surely not be forgotten.

Now come along with me as we enter the grand theater for our preview showing of "SIGMUND SAYS."

As you make yourself comfortable, the lights dim, the curtains slowly open, und as they say in show business, let's get on with the show.

What they also say is: no smoking, no loud talking, eat a lot of candy und popcorn, und have a nice time. But please, no gum under the seats.

SIGMUND FREUD

PRESENTS

THE

PERSONALITY KIDS

ID, EGO, AND SUPER-EGO

In this movie you will come in contact with some famous actors und actresses. I will introduce them to you. First though, let me tell you about the exciting parts I play in this film. As the head man, I have given myself a dual role, not to be confused with a split personality (although all of this could give someone a splitting headache if they are not careful).

In my first role, I am the professor und teacher, a part not at all unfamiliar to me. In my other role, I am the film's translator. As the translator, I will explain what some of the strange language in this movie means (that is, if I can figure it out myself). Confused yet? Keep reading, it's bound to happen.

In foreign films, English sub-titles are used so people can understand what's happening. In this film, I will place an asterisk (*) next to some of the foreign words *und will include my translator's notes explaining what is being said.

Here's your first sub-title (translation):

> *und = when you say "and" it may sound that way to you, but with my accent, well, it comes out like "und," und that's the way it is

Now that we have gotten past all of that *malarkey, I will introduce you to the other major "characters" in this **extravaganza. First, we have the two leading stars, who may look familiar to you.

They are:

SHE   und   HE
und you und me

*malarkey = a lot of idol chit chat und insignificant stuff
**extravaganza = this ***wunderbar film
***wunderbar = wonderful

Speaking of characters, I call the other three stars the personality kids, because they make up the three systems of our personality. Their names are: Id (sounds like Sid, leave off the S und we've got Id), Ego und Super-Ego.

The Id is a cute little guy, isn't he? But be careful, because this kid is the spoiled child of our personality. Like a newborn baby, all Id cares about is satisfying our needs without concern for anything or anybody else. Fun und pleasure are his only goals. It may not sound too bad to you, but remember: man does not live by fun alone.

Next is the Ego, who is the executive und coordinator of our personality. Ego tries to control the Id's *impulsive behavior und provide some reality und balance for the **goot of our whole personality. Have you ever tried to control an impulsive Id? It ain't easy.

When problems come up (und who doesn't have problems), Ego tries to solve them in a logical way with real solutions in mind. Ego is like the adult part of our personality.

---

*impulsive = spur of the moment action without prior thoughts of what might happen because of what we do

**goot = you say good, I say goot, whatever way we say it, it's not bad

Last, but not least, we have our Super-Ego. As the moral und judicial part of our personality, Super-Ego thinks everyone should be as super as he is. This kid could push us toward *perfection und beyond, if we let him.

Super-Ego wants us to conform to all the wishes our parents ever had for us. While learning from our parents what's right und what's wrong und growing up to be goot people is important for us, Super-Ego overdoes it. He can be extremely judgmental of everyone und everything und that's why we call this part of us the judge.

*perfection = they don't come any better

As I said before, these kids make up the three major systems of our personality. Sometimes they play nice together und at times they each want their own way.

Now I will explain how these three kids work both separately und together to become the organization of our personality. In other words, what makes us tick.

**ID
EGO
und
SUPER-EGO**

In the emotionally healthy person, the Id, Ego und Super-Ego come together und form a harmonious group. Like with a goot orchestra, when everyone plays in tune together, the music can sound wunderbar.

When they work together in a nice way they allow you und
me to satisfy our basic needs und desires. In other words,
we make beautiful music together.

However, when they don't play together in harmony, it's
*ach und vey und **maladjustment in you or me occurs.

```
*ach und vey = it's too bad und it's not so goot
                    for you or me
**maladjustment = problem adjusting to the
                    environment
```

Now it's time to explain how each of these three systems works. Are you ready? Well, ready or not, here we go.

Once again I will begin with the Id (not because Id is my favorite, although he is kind of cute; but like a goot father figure I don't play favorites).

The Id is not affected by our ability to use reasoning or logic und he doesn't have any ethical or moral values either. He's something else, as they say in modern talk. This Id kid is motivated by only one thing: to satisfy our needs according to the PLEASURE PRINCIPLE.

WELL, I'LL TELL YOU
UND I'M GLAD
YOU ASKED.

The purpose or aim of the pleasure principle is to get rid of pain und *tension. The Id does this by trying to substitute satisfaction und **pleasure for any situation that might be painful. The Id works at helping people feel better, even if it's only temporarily. This is one of the Id's main jobs. Sounds goot, right? But I warn you, don't ***jump to conclusions.

*tension = negative energy that builds up, causing pain
            und discomfort
**pleasure = how goot it feels when you feel goot
***jump to conclusions = when judging too quickly, one's
            answers may be inaccurate und disappointing

The Id is in closer contact with our body und how we react und feel than with the outside world (which consists of those actions und situations which affect us). The Id cannot handle waiting for changes to take place; he wants what he wants when he wants it, which is usually right now. Like when we were babies, we demanded to be changed und fed when we felt the time was right.

Id stays in its own little world und is not aware of what I call *OBJECTIVE REALITY.

*objective reality = *"It's the real thing"*

So how does Id do this? *Kommen sie hier, und I'll tell you.

*kommen sie hier = come closer

The Id does not consider what might happen as a result of what it does. Operating only from *instinct, the main thing Id understands is: stop the pain und produce pleasure.

*instinct = a powerful impulse that comes from within

If you or I were to function with only our Id, we wouldn't deal too well with any of life's situations that didn't bring us pleasure. We would spend all our time trying to escape from everything that causes pain, discomfort or isn't fun.

On the other hand, und their usually is another hand, the Id is also an important part of us. That fact should become clear when we understand that the Id is the *reservoir of our mind's energy und furnishes the power to keep the other two systems in operation. Und what do you think about that?

*reservoir = a large supply of something

The Id has a problem with being the major supplier of energy, because when the Id's supply of energy increases, this energy feels like tension. Und you know how the Id reacts to anything uncomfortable. So, the Id does what we might expect: when the level of tension in the *organism goes up, the Id discharges it und brings the energy level back down to what is comfortable.

Again, this is what the pleasure principle is all about: if what's happening doesn't feel goot (uncomfortable or unpleasant), get rid of it or change it.

*organism = any living individual or thing

How does the pleasure principle work? That's what I call a goot question. Now all we need is a goot answer.

Our Id, wanting to avoid pain und to provide pleasure, uses two processes. The first is called REFLEX ACTION. This is *inborn und is an automatic reaction, which is what happens when you und I sneeze or blink. We don't plan it, we just do it. The reflex action reduces tension immediately und the tickle in the nose goes with it.

HAH-CHU!**

*inborn = something we are born with, instead of learning
**hah-chu = it's a goot sneeze und may produce a ***spritzer
***spritzer = like a seltzer spray without the bottle und
              without the seltzer

The second process which the little Id kid uses to avoid pain is the PRIMARY PROCESS. I also call it WISH FULFILLMENT.

If you or me, he or she, were on a desert island without any *wasser, with our Id's help, we might **dream some up. This is wish fulfillment; making our wishes come true in our mind, even if it isn't real.

*wasser = what you call water
**dream some up = mirage or illusion
***  = mental image of wasser

These wish fulfilling images are the only kind of reality Id understands, und thirsty you und me can't drink images.

*oy vey = how painful it is

Pretty soon you will learn how the Ego uses the SECONDARY PROCESS to offset the Id's primary process. Sometimes it works und sometimes it doesn't.

That's enough with the Id. Now I'll tell you about the number two partner, the Ego.

The Ego handles all of the transactions between you und me und the world we live in.

*vot a bizness = it isn't easy handling the whole world

The Ego operates under und is controlled by the REALITY PRINCIPLE. The reality principle's prime purpose is to postpone or delay the discharge of energy by the Id until the actual object to satisfy the need is found or produced.

When we operate under the reality principle, instead of attempting to drink an illusion (like in the pleasure principle), we try to get the real stuff.

*wasser stand = that's where the colorless cool liquid (wasser) is, und if you have some in the desert, it tastes very goot

The Ego must ensure that tension is *tolerated, und any action postponed until the tension can be discharged by an **appropriate behavior. Ever try to hold back a horse full of get up und go? Well, that's what it's like to harness the Id.

*tolerate = put up with or handle something or somebody that ain't so easy to put up with or handle
**appropriate behavior = when people act as I think they should act, that is appropriate behavior

The Ego temporarily suspends the pleasure principle in the interest of reality, und that's not easy.

The Ego runs the SECONDARY PROCESS. This is the problem solving or thinking part, und starts when the Id, through its primary process, produces a picture of a need.

The major difference between the Id und Ego is: The Id only operates with *SUBJECTIVE REALITY of the mind, und the Ego knows the difference between those things we create through dreams in our minds und those things that are real in the **external world.

```
*subjective reality = what appears as real in a person's
        mind; not affected by what goes on in the real
        (external) world
**external world = the world we live in, which includes
        others besides ourselves
```

DREAMS

REALITY

Let me tell you it ain't an easy job for the Ego, und teaching is not so easy either.

As our story continues, it should be remembered that the Ego is the organized part of the Id und its purpose is to help the Id accomplish its goals, not control them.

Also remember that all the energy und power comes from the Id. The Ego's main role is to *mediate the Id's energy between our instinctual needs und the real conditions of our environment. The Ego's goal is to ensure that our lives go on und to make sure that the **species is reproduced.

*mediate = to effect an acceptable agreement that works
**species = a lot of new you und me und everyone else

OOPS! The film has come apart at the seams. Hopefully the information in my lecture will hold together a little better.

When the film breaks, the Id says we take a break too. The Ego, on the other hand, will try to paste the film together, und the Super-Ego wants to know who did it. After this unexpected intermission, I will return with the Super-Ego.

Now that the film has been put together, I will pull myself together und tell you about the number three partner, the Super-Ego.

The Super-Ego is the independent part of our personality. Und is he independent. He tries to make everything right, as he sees it, und will let you know when anything is wrong.

The Super-Ego gets energy from the Ego (who gets it from the Id) und the Super-Ego tries to dominate the Ego with his strict moral standards. Often the Super-Ego uses his energy to overpower the Ego with feelings of guilt. I don't think we need to translate guilt; it feels the same in all languages.

The Super-Ego got all of its learning during the time when you und I und the whole gang of us were *kinder. During those early days, our **ma ma und ***da da said, "Do this und do that und this is goot und that is ****schlecht."

```
*kinder = children
**ma ma = mother
***da da = father
****schlecht = bad, which ain't too goot
```

Through rewards und punishment, the parents (yours und mine) established *TRADITIONAL VALUES for us kinder.

The Super-Ego, being the moral arm of the personality, insists that we follow the traditional values of our parents und all other authority figures.

*traditional values = thoughts und behaviors passed on from generation to generation

The Super-Ego also functions with two sub-systems. One is the *CONSCIENCE (the punishment part), which speaks to us from within und tells us:

"You should do this und you shouldn't do that."

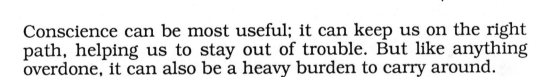

Conscience can be most useful; it can keep us on the right path, helping us to stay out of trouble. But like anything overdone, it can also be a heavy burden to carry around.

The Super-Ego through the conscience tries to <u>stop</u> the Id's impulses, whereas the Ego tries to <u>delay</u> them.

*conscience = can punish us by **making us feel bad
**making us feel bad = guilt

The Super-Ego's other system is called EGO-IDEAL. The ego-ideal is the rewarding part or opposite of the conscience (which is the punishing part).

The ego-ideal seeks idealistic or perfect goals und also perfect outcomes for these goals. When we attain our goals, the ego-ideal rewards us by making us feel goot for being goot und it presents us with feelings of pride as the payment for our accomplishment.

*snoring = ZZZZ

Super-Ego sees to it that parental control becomes self-control, und that the Id's sexual und aggressive impulses are *inhibited.

*inhibited = for Super-Ego it means: stopped

Our uncontrolled sexual und aggressive impulses imposed upon others are most highly condemned by *society, und are therefore condemned by the Super-Ego as well.

The Super-Ego also makes sure that its moralistic goals become people's realistic goals. This is done by putting a lot of pressure on the Ego to adopt these as realistic goals.

In other words, The Super-Ego's desire is to reshape the world in its own image, as it thinks everything und everybody should be. This is the Super-Ego's major focus.

As we bring the three kids (our personality systems) together, we see that the Id, who is the source of our energy supply, has only a limited amount of it. When one of the three systems becomes more powerful (with energy), the other two systems are weakened.

If you or I are controlled by our Id, we will be impulsive in our behavior und not too concerned about practical things.

If empowered by the Id, we would not deal too well with difficult situations, such as conflict or any other kind of problems. Instead, we would prefer to remain childlike: escaping und resisting life's complexities, und whenever we can, finding other people to take care of us.

If we are controlled by the Ego, we would be more
*pragmatic und would concern ourselves with being
practical und realistic. With a dominant Ego, having fun is
less important than facing the more serious side und the
reality of life.

| *pragmatic = seeks practical results |

If the Super-Ego is in charge, we would be highly moralistic, always looking at everything as right or wrong und black or white. We may also measure everyone else by our own rigid standards. Those dominated by the Super-Ego are burdened by guilt und attempt to pass it on to others as well.

What works best for your personality und mine, would be to have a balance of the three systems. Then we can be spontaneous und fun loving (with the Id's help), know right from wrong (thanks to the Super-Ego), und establish realistic goals to improve our lives (through our Ego).

Und now my class, for those of you who are still awake, I have an announcement to make. With this lecture coming to its conclusion, I have but one more important thing to say to you —

*class dismissed = I have run out of time und patience

I am sorry to tell you viewers that this show is also over. I hope this film has been enjoyable und informative for you. I also hope that you may understand your personality und the personality kids within you a little better than you did before. Und who knows, maybe now your Id, Ego und Super-Ego will learn to play sweeter music together.

As the curtains close, to you my friends I say: *auf Wiedersehen.

*auf Wiedersehen = good-bye or until we meet again

FINIS

This screening was approved for all audiences willing to sit through it.

Any similarity between the characters in this story und real live characters, except for you und me, is too bad.

* * *

Produced by Sigmund Films
with a lot of help from Monroe Press

We gratefully acknowledge and say thanks to the following for helping to keep our facts straight:

Eidelberg, Ludwig, M.D., Ed. *Encyclopedia of Psychoanalysis.* New York: The Free Press, 1968.

Freud, Sigmund. *The Ego and The Id.* Trans. Joan Riviere. Ed. James Strachey. New York: W.W. Norton & Company, Inc. 1960.

Goldenson, Robert M., Ph.D. *The Encyclopedia of Human Behavior: Psychology, Psychiatry, and Mental Health.* Garden City: Doubledey & Company, Inc., 1970.

Hall, Calvin S. *A Primer of Freudian Psychology.* New York: The New American Library, Inc., 1954.

Mullahy, Patrick. *Oedipus Myth & Complex.* New York: Hermitage House Inc., 1953.

OTHER BOOKS BY THE AUTHOR

Why Can't Anyone Hear Me?
 A Guide for Surviving Adolescence

Teacher/Counselor Guide to Adolescent Enrichment
 A Teen Issues and Self/Esteem Improvement Program

Teen Issues Workbook

Stress Reduction Training - Audio tape

Working Together - Participative management video tape

A MESSAGE FROM THE AUTHOR

It has been my pleasure to share *SIGMUND SAYS* with you. I hope that you have enjoyed it. If you care to share any of your thoughts or feelings about the book with me, I would be pleased to hear from you. Send your comments to Monroe Press at the address below.

SPECIAL ORDER INFORMATION

Additional copies of *SIGMUND SAYS*, and other materials by Dr. Elchoness, may be ordered through your local book store or directly from Monroe Press, 16107 Gledhill Street, #188, Sepulveda, CA 91343-2918. (818) 891-6464.

Sigmund Says	$6.95
Why Can't Anyone Hear Me?	10.95
* *Guide to Adolescent Enrichment*	14.95
* *Teen Issues Workbook*	4.95
Stress Reduction Training (audio tape)	9.00

* For use with *Why Can't Anyone Hear Me?*

Include $1.50 shipping/handling for first book, and $1.00 for each additional book. California residents add 6% tax.